THE
POWER GAME
POCKET
COMPANION

THE
POWER GAME
POCKET
COMPANION

Proven Tips on How to
Reach Your Power Potential

JIM MCLEAN AND **JOHN ANDRISANI**

HarperCollins*Publishers*

HarperCollins books may be purchased for educational, business, or sales promotional use. For information, please write to: Special Markets Department, HarperCollins Publishers, Inc., 10 East 53rd Street, New York, New York 10022.

FIRST EDITION

Designed by Ruth Lee

Library of Congress Cataloging-in-Publication Data

McLean, Jim.
    The power game pocket companion : proven tips on how to reach your power potential / by Jim McLean and John Andrisani. —1st ed.
        p.   cm.
    ISBN 0-06-273470-9
    1. Swing (Golf) 2. Golf—Drive. I. Andrisani, John. II. Title.
GV979.S9M325 1996
796.352'3—dc21   96-52253

97 98 99 00 01 ❖/HC 10 9 8 7 6 5 4 3 2 1

INTRODUCTION

Golfers are finding out that even the most technologically advanced equipment, such as the new Callaway "Great Big Bertha" and the Taylor Made "Bubble," can't help them reach their maximum power potential.

There are two chief criteria for hitting the ball with power and control: clubhead speed and square clubface-to-ball contact. Unless you are blessed with exceptional strength, superb feel, and phenomenal hand-eye coordination, plus have hours to devote to practice, the only way to achieve these goals is to develop a technically sound power swing. (Only extremely talented players can get away with a highly unorthodox swing.) To do that you must start by learning the vital elements of the power address, power backswing, and power downswing. Developing a power swing is one sure way to beat the course. As the great Ben Hogan said, "If you can't drive the ball far and straight, you can't play the tournament golf."

Although designers are finally moving away from the 7,000-yard courses, first made popular during the 1970s, golf courses are still too long for the average golfer. The average club-level player has great difficulty hitting most par-4 and par-5 holes in regulation figures. Furthermore, many long par-3s require the golfer to hit the ball powerfully enough to carry it over a mammoth water hazard or ravine, all the way to the green.

So go the frustrations of golfers. Which explains, to a large degree, why Mr. and Ms. Average can't break 100. It's also one big reason why "10 More Yards," a new column in *GOLF Magazine,* is the best "draw" instruction page. It's the reason, too, why sales of balls promising extra length have skyrocketed. Power has always been an attractive subject. But now it truly is hot.

The average player is aware of the importance of the short game and putting. But he's even more aware that with a longer tee shot, a shorter, more lofted club for the approach shot into the green is a great reward. That means more chances at hitting the ball close to the hole and shooting a good score. Besides scoring advantages, the excitement of hitting a long tee shot straight down the middle of the fairway, over a hazard, or around a dogleg, is far more thrilling than chipping or pitching a ball into the hole, or even sinking a very long putt.

The problem is, the typical club player hits too few long or straight drives due largely to poor technique. The bottom line: The average player is rarely going to hit a long drive. That shouldn't be the case. Players should build a power swing that is reliable, or be given a high number of long driving tips and hints, so that they can experiment and determine which ones work best.

In *The Power Game Pocket Companion,* we offer 100 unique instructional tips, with accompanying photographs that more clearly help relay the instructional message. These original power-driving tips are all quick and easy to follow. Therefore, you don't have to read a long text or understand a completely new swing theory just to learn something that will add 10 to 20 yards to your tee shots. Simply, test one tip, then move on to the next. There is something here for every golfer.

These tips come from our own experience and knowledge in golf, and in working with some of the game's greatest teachers and tour professionals.

Good luck in your quest for power. We know that you're only one tip away from that elusive super solid tee shot. Here's to 10 more yards!

—Jim McLean and John Andrisani

PART ONE

THE POWER GAME

BY JIM MCLEAN

TIP #1:
INCREASE MPH OF
CENTER ROTATION

One of the unknown secrets of increasing clubhead speed is improving the pivot action. That means rotating your body center faster in the downswing. Once the middle part of your body increases mph, then your arms and clubs can pick up the pace as well.

TIP #2:
TEE IT HIGH, LET IT FLY!

This old saying is actually right on the mark. I suggest you take it literally. That means tee your golf ball extra high at address—à la Chi Chi Rodriguez—with at least half of the ball above the clubface or even higher. In addition, move the ball position forward to about your left instep. This sets you well behind the ball at address and encourages a slight upswing into impact. By picking the ball off on the upswing, you can learn to flatten the trajectory of your tee shot. The ball gets up quickly, then flattens out into a line drive, the perfect launch. Remember to really let go. Hit with total abandonment.

A high tee position will promote a powerful upswing-hit.

TIP #3:
MOVE YOUR LEFT FOOT FORWARD (CREATE LEFT LEG ANGLE)

At address, place your left foot well outside your left shoulder. This little-known tip can add a lot of power to your swing. First, it widens your stance and provides a powerful base. Second, and most importantly, this left foot positioning allows you to make a powerful lateral move into a straight braced left leg. This is often referred to as "hitting into your left side." After impact, the left leg is straight and you grow into a tall finish with perfect balance. Remember, the key is left foot positioning.

TIP #4:
TURN THE LEFT TOE OUT

At address, be sure to turn the toe end of your left foot out at least 30 degrees, like all power hitters. This position allows you to increase the speed of your hip rotation through the ball, while it actually decreases the hip turn and leg action in the backswing. Both of these actions are highly desirable.

Turn the left foot outward, to increase the speed of your hip rotation through impact.

TIP #5:
LOAD, UNLOAD, EXPLODE!

To hit long, your body must move in the correct sequence. The correct sequence is to *load* on the backswing by coiling into your back leg, *unload* by starting the downswing from the ground up with a weight shift and rotation, *explode* by letting go with your entire right side.

On the backswing, the key is to "load" up your power.

TIP #6:
ARMS ARE ROPES

Visualize that your arms are like two ropes hanging off your body—absolutely tension free. Maintain this image of two ropes throughout the swing. If you do, the weight of the club will maintain full extension of your arms and you will develop a very powerful swing powered by the body. The arms are put into action as a result of your body action, not vice versa—a great visual image especially in competition.

*Imagining your arms as ropes, hanging off your body,
will help you relax your muscles and
employ a more powerful swinging action.*

TIP #7:
MUSCLE POWER

To stretch and strengthen your golf muscles, so that you're able to hit the ball powerfully, practice swinging a broom about ten times daily.

Swinging a broom will stretch and strengthen your golf muscles.

TIP #8:
SIMPLE HIP–TURNING KEY

Take a page out of Greg Norman's lesson book. He thinks RHP (right hip pocket) to encourage a clockwise turning action of the right hip on the backswing. The stronger the winding action of your right hip, the more power you will unleash into the ball (once that hip unwinds on the downswing).

*Think of turning your right hip away from
the target to promote a power swing.*

TIP #9:
SHAFT TO SHOULDER

Legendary teacher Harry Cooper would often have his students increase clubhead speed by focusing on hitting their left shoulder with the shaft, at the completion of the swing. This lower finish increased speed dramatically. Think of a Davis Love, Fred Couples or Tiger Woods finish. Make your shaft hit your shoulder quickly, and you'll immediately pick up distance.

Trying to get the clubshaft to cross your left shoulder, in the finish, will promote a powerful through-swing.

TIP #10:
INCREASE YOUR GAP

Long hitters, most notably John Daly, get a bigger percentage of their turn from the upper body and shoulders. They turn their shoulders far more than their hips, and thus create a large gap between these two vital turning points. This creates torque, which most people feel in the upper left side. Like a wound-up spring, the golfer is now poised in a powerful coiled position. Try this in front of a mirror.

In swinging back, turn your shoulders more than your hips.

TIP #11:
INCREASE YOUR
SHOULDER TURN

To gain flexibility and increase a short shoulder turn, try the following exercise: Take a 5-iron and make your full backswing. Remember to keep your left heel on the ground, and also maintain some flex in your right knee. Hold your top-of-the-backswing position. Next, add another two or three degrees of turn. Hold that position. Then add another two or three degrees of shoulder turn. You will feel a lot of stretch in your upper left side. Through repetition, you will gradually increase your flexibility and shoulder turn.

TIP #12:
INCREASE YOUR LAG

Baseball great and World Series MVP Ralph Terry showed my sons a great baseball hitting drill. It was a check-swing where the boys held the bat back as they made the stride toward the pitch. Ralph stayed with me during the Senior PGA Tour event I hosted at Sleepy Hollow Country Club in New York. Ralph was one of the few athletes to compete in two professional sports. I then applied Ralph's check-swing baseball drill to golf. It's simple. From the top of your backswing, make the strongest move down toward the ball, only check your swing. Hold the angle you had at the top. Stop your swing at waist-high level. It's a tremendous drill for helping you learn to wait. Repeat it often.

Freezing the lag-position will make you a stronger ball striker.

TIP #13:
WHO SHOULD
RELEASE EARLIER

If you tend to slice or block the ball, you probably pull the grip end of the club too much, or open the shoulders much too fast on the downswing. Therefore, try releasing the right arm and club downward immediately from the top of the backswing, before your shoulders can initiate a turning action. Jack Nicklaus always preached an early release, as long as you had the legs and lower body leading the action.

TIP #14:
THE "ATTACK TRACK"

I've used this term to preach the correct path of the power swing. Long hitters attack the golf ball, but they swing on a proper plane and hit the ball from inside the target line. This gives them flush contact into the back of the ball (actually just a micro-fraction to the inside of the ball). You need to visualize this inside attack and practice it constantly. Make numerous practice swings in front of a mirror to master this vital move.

Power hitters attack the ball from a shallow inside path.

TIP #15:
LOWER YOUR
CENTER OF GRAVITY

At address, brace yourself off the inside part of your legs until you feel your center of gravity lower. This feeling of grounding yourself puts you into a super athletic setup, similar to a linebacker in football. From this position you can use the earth to push off. It's a great feeling of power.

*An athletic set-up will promote a
technically-sound power swing.*

TIP #16:
FREE UP YOUR
RIGHT ELBOW

At address, many amateurs tuck their right elbow against their right side. This faulty setup position prevents you from employing a powerful wind-up action. Instead, relax the right arm and make sure it hangs free of your body with the right elbow a hand length off your right hip. That will help you to hit much longer drives. So, keep your right arm relaxed at address, and free from your body.

*At address, it's best to keep your right arm relaxed
and away from your body.*

TIP #17:
LEVEL YOUR FOREARMS

At address, the most powerful and natural arm position will find your forearms parallel to the target line. Don't allow your right forearm to be either under or over your left forearm at address. A line drawn across your forearms should line up with your feet, knees, hips, and shoulders.

TIP #18:
TILT YOUR SPINE

At address, tilt your spine approximately 10 degrees away from the target. You can do this most naturally by taking a fairly wide stance and playing the ball forward, off your left heel. Since your right hand is lower on the grip, this will put your right shoulder lower than your left shoulder with no effort on your part. This set-up puts you in position to strike the ball slightly on the upswing; the perfect angle of attack for producing powerful shots.

You can tell from the angle of the buttons on my shirt that I've correctly tilted my spine away from the target. Copy this same starting position to promote a strong hit on the upswing.

TIP #19:
LEVEL ELBOWS AT THE TOP

Check to see if your elbows are level—equal height off the ground—as you reach the top of your backswing. To many golfers, this position seems awkward, yet it is the position achieved by most long hitters. If you feel your right elbow is flying to achieve this position, take a look at Fred Couples, John Daly, or Jack Nicklaus. Their right elbow is actually higher than the left elbow at the top. This position provides tremendous leverage.

TIP #20:
CONNECT THE LEFT ARM

At address, the upper left arm must touch the upper left side (pec region) of your body.

The best idea I've ever heard in golf to communicate this is top teacher Jimmy Ballard's concept of "plugging in." Ballard uses this image of plugging your upper left arm into a socket in the left side of your body. Further, he tells students to maintain this power connection throughout the swing. So should you.

Set up with your upper left arm "connected" to the pectoral-muscle region of your body.

TIP #21:
BEND THE RIGHT ELBOW

At address, slightly bend the right arm at the elbow. This relaxes your right arm, shoulder, and hand. One of the most critical aspects of creating speed is relaxed muscles. To throw a fastball, the first thing a major league pitcher does is relax his arm. Tense muscles mean slow speed.

TIP #22:
EXTEND YOUR LEFT ARM

At address, make sure your left arm is fully extended, providing the greatest radius possible to the ball. Although the left arm must not be tense or rigid, it must be at full length. A bent or short left arm setup position will cause you to pull up and out of the shot through impact. So extend it, to promote power.

It's important to establish a strong radius at address,
so keep your left arm straight.

TIP #23:
ARMS HANG OUT, NOT
STRAIGHT DOWN

The worst position possible for power is to have your arms hang straight down, or worse yet, inward from the shoulder sockets. Make sure your arms hang at an angle, down to the grip. For a driver, I like the left hand directly under the eye line. This creates a substantial gap between your hands and your body. In turn, this gap helps you swing the driver on a proper plane, and also gives your hands room to swing with no interference from the body.

TIP #24:
RIGHT HAND TO RIGHT SHOULDER

To gain leverage and speed, check your right hand to right shoulder gap at the top of your swing. Many golfers lose the width of their swing at the top by allowing the right hand to collapse toward the right shoulder. Don't make this mistake. Have in mind the image of a string connecting your right hand to your right shoulder at the top of your backswing. Don't allow that string to collapse. Keep your width.

TIP #25:
THE RIGHT ARM "L"

As you complete your backswing your right arm will fold at the elbow. The upper arm and the forearm will eventually form the letter "L." The problem I see is that many golfers continue to fold the right arm excessively and end up forming the letter "V." This causes a major power leak. Your extension diminishes, and the left arm is forced to bend excessively. Check to see if you keep the letter "L" at the top of the backswing.

At the top of the swing, the right forearm
and upper arms should form an L.

TIP #26:
TWO PIVOT POINTS

To hit for power, forget about the old concept of a fixed center or single pivot point. There are two pivot points in a power golf swing. Pivot around your right leg on the backswing, then shift into your left leg on the downswing. Allow your head to rotate and move with the pivot.

This full-balanced finish indicates that the player has pivoted nicely around the left leg on the downswing.

TIP #27:
BODY ANGLES AT THE TOP
(THE X–FACTOR)

When you reach the top of your backswing, ask yourself these questions. Have you shifted at least 75 percent of your weight onto the right leg? Have you turned your shoulders far more than your hips? Is your left shoulder over the inside part of your right leg? Has your head shifted a few inches to the right? If you answered yes to these questions, you're employing all the vital power moves of a power backswing, and you have created a large X—the differential between shoulder turn and hip turn.

TIP #28:
SLOW, SLOW, SLOW

I always remember Jack Nicklaus talking and writing about a slow takeaway when he wanted to hit the ball farther. In all of my teaching, I've found this to be absolutely true. When you are going to reach for a little extra, never allow yourself to speed up the takeaway. Instead, slow down to gather all your force and strength. It works.

In triggering a power swing,
it's critical to start the club away slowly.

TIP #29:
LOWER THE "L"

From the top of the backswing, allow your right arm to fall or lower as you initiate the move down to impact. By lowering the right shoulder, the L-position of the right arm (which is formed at the top of the backswing) remains intact deep into the downswing. With no effort to pull the club down, you can still maintain tremendous lag. If you straighten the right arm "L" prematurely, you lose a tremendous power source.

TIP #30:
SWING LIKE AN ATHLETE

I teach an athletic move in golf which corresponds to all powerful throwing or hitting actions. To hit with power, you must follow this natural athletic sequence of movements the split second you reach the top of the backswing. The first move must be lateral (shift). As you shift center, the right shoulder will respond by lowering. The next move is rotational. That means center turns through impact. Finally, the throw of the arms and hands occurs, beginning approximately at the waist-high position. If you start down properly, you can hit hard. However if you rotate or throw first, you'll never hit the ball with maximum power. Practice the correct throwing sequence. Shift, rotate, hit.

TIP #31:
TWENTY–TWENTY

I learned this power drill from my first teacher, Al Mengert. It's a great one for building speed and balance into your swing. Use a driver and make twenty full swings in a row. Keep swinging (both ways: left and right). Keep your heels low to the ground as you make these continuous swings. This helps you level out your swing and develop a tension-free power action.

*Making 20 full swings in a row will help you develop a
tension-free power action.*

TIP #32:
FOUR POWER SOURCES

There are four main sources of power that I feel you should consider.

1. The wrists: which cock and uncock. (The left wrist also flattens, or bows, through impact.)
2. The arms: which swing and remain relaxed throughout the swing.
3. Your weight shift: which provides lateral drive and increased power.
4. Your body turn: which provides incredible leverage and speed.

We must use all four power sources in order to maximize our full power potential.

The turning action of your body is a strong power source.

TIP #33:
BODY ANGLES AT ADDRESS

At address, set yourself up for a powerful hit by positioning yourself correctly. Keep your chin off your chest, but have relaxed neck muscles. Bend from the waist so that your hip pockets are four to eight inches outside your heels. Flex your knees slightly, but maintain maximum height. The body should be perfectly balanced with weight equally distributed on both feet. The right shoulder should set lower than the left shoulder, but be careful not to overdo this. A line drawn across the top of your shoulders should not exceed 20 degrees.

TIP #34:
ONE SURE KEY
FOR GROOVING
A SMOOTH SWING

To learn to swing "within yourself" and hit the ball with controlled power, practice hitting shots with your feet together. If you swing too fast, you'll feel yourself lose your balance.

*This feet-together drill will help
you learn to "swing within yourself."*

TIP #35:
VIDEOTAPE CHECKPOINT

To check that you're in the ideal downswing power position, have a friend videotape your swing. As you start down, the butt end of the club should point at the target line. Make sure the butt end of the club is not pointed at a line between the target line and your foot line indicating a steep and weak angle of attack.

TIP #36:
SWING WITH ABANDON

To promote a free swing—one free of any inhibitions—pretend you're hitting into the Atlantic Ocean, or a big lake. The great Jackie Burke Jr. gave me that tip. It's a great swing thought on tight holes or for tournament play. When feeling like they are hitting into a very open area, most people make their best swing.

*Pretending you're hitting into a big lake
will help you swing with abandon.*

TIP #37:
GO ON–LINE

All long hitters reach the same position at the halfway point on the downswing. When the player's hands are level with his right thigh, the clubshaft is parallel to the target line. The clubface is perpendicular to the target line.

To get into this power delivery position, practice in front of a mirror. Many people are helped by closing the stance and body alignment slightly, and then keeping the right elbow close to the body on the downswing.

TIP #38:
THE INSIDE STORY

An inside-square-inside clubhead path is the most powerful. If your ball position and body motions are correct, and the arms stay in front of your chest throughout the swing, the club *must* swing on a powerful inside-to-inside arc.

It's critical to swing the club along an inside path, while keeping your arms in front of your body.

TIP #39:
SQUEEZE PLAYS

One key to generating power in the golf swing is developing strength and suppleness in your hands and arms. An easy way to accomplish this goal is to squeeze a rubber ball in each hand five minutes at a time. Senior PGA Tour sensation and golf great Gary Player still does this exercise regularly.

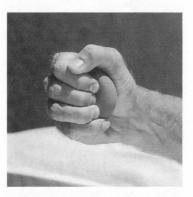

Squeezing a rubber ball will help strengthen vital muscles in your hands and arms.

TIP #40:
KEEP THE TOE UP

In a sound power swing, the toe of the club should point skyward at the halfway point of the backswing. The clubface can be slightly closed but never rolled open at this checkpoint. Practice until you groove this vital position, as it practically ensures a proper top of the backswing position.

At this point in the swing, the toe of the club should point toward the sky.

TIP #41:
MIND GAME

To help you hit through the ball with added power, pretend there's a second ball, teed up two inches in front of the "real" one. Hit the imaginary ball, and the real one will be a long way down the fairway before you know it.

To promote powerful contact, imagine you have to hit through your ball to hit an imaginary one, teed up in front of it.

TIP #42:
THANKS, MOE

To help you keep the clubhead low to the ground, and employ a one-piece takeaway, set the club down about a foot behind the ball, as Canadian pro Moe Norman does. This gets you away perfectly. Great for golfers who lift the club abruptly or over-extend the left arm.

TIP #43:
PERFECT IMPACT

Here are some vital points you must understand about impact in order to groove a power swing:

1. The body's weight is at least 75 percent to the left side;
2. The hands are well out in front of the address alignment;
3. The left wrist is flat;
4. The right heel is off the ground;
5. The right knee is kicking forward at the ball;
6. The hips are turned well left, about 30 degrees;
7. The shoulders should be slightly open to the target line;
8. The head is behind the ball;
9. The sweet spot of the clubface is dead square to the ball.

The most vital position of all: impact.

TIP #44:
PRACTICE MAKES PERFECT

The next time you step up to the side of the ball, taking a practice swing, don't just sort of waggle the club. Take a serious swing, trying to generate high clubhead speed, and hit an imaginary ball.

Make your practice swing count.

TIP #45:
UP AGAINST THE BALL

If an overly flat swing is causing you to block the ball—and lose distance—practice swinging near a wall. Practice until you can swing back without the clubhead hitting the wall.

TIP #46:
HEEL TRIGGER

Always use some slight motion to trigger the takeaway. I recommend a lifting and replanting of the right heel as one way to initiate motion.

*You may want to use this heel-trigger
to promote a powerful swing.*

TIP #47:
PUSH OFF
THE RIGHT INSTEP

One key Sam Snead used for extra distance in his driving game was the thought of initiating the forward swing with a right foot image. As you begin your move down and then through the golf shot, focus on your right instep. Think of the inside part of your right foot rolling toward the target as you approach impact—heel leading toe. It's similar to a baseball pitcher pushing off of the rubber to gain leverage. Snead felt this push off the right instep helped him drive through the shot for extra distance. Give it a try.

To program power into your action,
let the heel of your right foot lead the toe.

TIP #48:
RETAIN THE FLEX

In order that you don't stand up and disrupt the turning action of your body, make sure that during the backswing you retain the flex in your right knee.

In swinging back, it's critical to retain the flex in your right knee.

TIP #49:
USE YOUR HEAD

In any good power swing, the chin rotates to the right and/or the head shifts slightly away from the target. If you need proof that this works, watch any long ball hitter in slow motion or stop action video.

In any good backswing, the head swivels away from the target.

TIP #50:
OPEN UP YOUR LEFT HIP

One of the secrets to increasing clubhead speed and delivering the sweet spot of the clubface squarely into the back center portion of the ball, is clearing your left hip on the downswing. Assuming an open alignment pre-clears the left hip, and ensures solid contact.

An open alignment will "pre-clear" the left hip.

PART TWO

THE
POWER
GAME

BY JOHN ANDRISANI

TIP #51:
A GAME OF INCHES

If you're a senior player looking to gain more distance off the tee, try using a driver that's an inch longer than standard; i.e., 45 inches, instead of 44. Your local pro can fit you.

The longer club helps you create a bigger swing arc, thereby allowing you to generate more clubhead speed and power at impact.

TIP #52:
HOW TO RELEASE
YOUR POWER

Those of you who lose distance because of a slice, probably fail to release the club correctly in the impact zone. If this is your problem, use a club with a thinner grip. This will enhance your hands-forearms releasing action, and allow you to deliver the sweet spot of the clubface squarely and more powerfully into the ball.

A thinner grip will help you release the club powerfully through impact, and arrive in a full finish position like this player is here.

TIP #53:
HOW TO BEAT THE WIND

When playing in wind, high handicap players often overswing. This fault causes you to lose balance and thus prevents you from hitting the ball powerfully.

To promote good balance and long tee shots, make a compact three-quarter-length backswing, John Cook style.

Try a shorter, more controlled swing, when playing in wind.

TIP #54:
WIDE STANCE
FOR WIDE ARC

Picking the club straight up into the air on the backswing is a fault that causes you to narrow the swing's arc and lose vital power. On the downswing, the tendency is to chop down and hit a high weak sky-ball.

To help you create a wide backswing arc and powerful sweeping action on the downswing, set up so that the distance between your feet is slightly wider than your shoulders.

*This extrawide stance will promote
a wide swing arc—and more power.*

TIP #55:
GET A GRIP

If a snap hook is costing you distance and accuracy off the tee, an overly strong grip could be to blame. This grip causes you to close the clubface at impact. In turn, you hit the ball with a dramatic right-to-left curve, and not very far.

To promote solid clubface-to-ball contact and longer, more accurate drives, make certain that when you look down, at address, the Vs formed by your thumbs and forefingers point midway between your chin and right shoulder.

TIP #56:
GET HIP

To increase clubhead speed and the distance you hit tee shots, turn your front hip briskly in a counterclockwise direction, at the start of the downswing. The great Ben Hogan was a master at making this move work wonders.

TIP #57:
TEE TIME

To promote a more powerful upswing hit, tilt the tee away from the target slightly.

TIP #58:
HEEL CONTROL

To increase the turning action of your hips and shoulders on the backswing, let your left heel lift up. Then, replant it on the downswing to trigger a powerful downswing action.

Allowing your left heel to lift off the ground can promote a stronger turning action.

TIP #59:
HOW TO TAME YOUR
TEMPO

If an overly fast swing produces wild shots, count "1" as you turn your shoulders on the backswing, "2" as you unwind your hips and swing down. This "numbers game" will help tame your quick tempo.

*To promote a smooth tempo, think "one"
as you make your backswing.*

TIP #60:
LONG DISTANCE DRILL

One of the very best drills I've ever used to gain distance is to move the ball a few inches forward from its normal driving position. In order to make contact, you will have to extend your arms extra long through impact. Hit 10 to 15 drives like this, and you'll quickly get the hang of the proper power-swing action.

The player's set-up for the "long distance" drill.

TIP #61:
POWER–FADE SECRETS

To hit a left-to-right power-fade shot, around the corner of a dogleg-right type hole:

1. Set up open (feet, knees, hips, and shoulders aiming left of target);
2. Swing the club back outside the target line;
3. Swing down across the target line.

The power-fade set-up.

TIP #62:
POWER–DRAW SECRETS

To hit a right-to-left power-draw shot:

1. Aim your body to the right of target (where you want the ball to start its flight);
2. Aim the clubface at your final target;
3. Swing normally.

The power-draw set-up.

TIP #63:
A LIGHT GRIP IS BEST

To promote a more fluid hands-arms-club release through impact, and more powerful tee shots, grip the club more lightly—3 on a 1–10 scale.

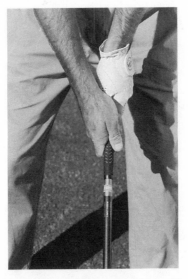

A lighter grip will promote more powerful release of the club.

TIP #64:
PLAY BALL

To help you stay behind the shot at impact, and contact the ball powerfully on the upswing, set up with the ball positioned forward in your stance.

Play the ball "up" to promote a powerful upswing-hit.

TIP #65:
CROSS THE LINE

If you want to be able to release your right hip, knee and shoulder, with no fear of coming over the top and slicing the shot, let the club swing across the line (clubshaft points directly at target) at the top.

This is what the cross-the-line position looks like.

TIP #66:
HOW TO GROOVE
A POWER SWING

To ingrain good power-swing positions into your muscle memory, practice swinging a weighted club.

TIP #67:
FINISH FIRST

Before you swing, visualize yourself in a balanced finish position. This mental image will encourage you to swing through the ball more powerfully.

To promote an accelerating swing, visualize a strong finish before your start the club back.

TIP #68:
SWING ON YOUR KNEES

To increase the flexibility in your shoulders, work on this drill at home:

Get down on your knees. Extend both arms and keep your palms about one foot apart. Now turn your left shoulder under your chin. Next, turn your right shoulder under your chin. Repeat at least 10 times a day for a week.

This exercise will increase the flexibility in your right shoulder and, ultimately, make you a stronger driver of the ball.

TIP #69:
RAPID–FIRE DRILL

If you block the ball right of target, your release action may be so slow that the clubface never squares itself to the target at impact. It finishes open.

To quicken your tempo slightly, line up a dozen teed-up balls. Step up to the first ball, swing, then keep right on going until all the balls have been struck. Don't give yourself time to dillydally or think too much about technique.

TIP #70:
A TURN FOR THE BEST

To promote a strong shoulder turn, one that will ultimately allow you to hit the ball powerfully, turn your left shoulder past the ball on the backswing.

*Rotate your left shoulder past the ball
to promote a strong shoulder turn.*

TIP #71:
THINK
"THROUGH THE BALL"

Visualize the fastest part of your swing past the ball. Like a karate blackbelt who will break several boards, you should think past or through your intended object. Sense extra speed past the ball; after impact and through to the finish. This mental key will promote solid club-to-ball penetration.

Seeing yourself hit past the ball will promote more powerful clubface-to-ball contact.

TIP #72:
WEIGHT SHIFT TIP

To promote a solid weight shift action into your right side on the backswing, set up with 60 percent of your weight on your right foot.

To promote a strong shifting action on the backswing, set up with 60 percent of your weight on your right foot.

TIP #73:
OUTWARD BOUND

Turn your right foot outward, approximately 20 degrees, to better allow your right hip to coil powerfully.

Turn your right foot outward to strengthen your hip-coil.

TIP #74:
MOVE 'EM BACK

Set your hands behind the ball slightly at address to encourage a wristless low takeaway action, and a wide powerful swing arc.

Set your hands behind the ball to promote a wide swing arc.

TIP #75:
HOW TO GROOVE A
WRISTLESS TAKEAWAY

A wristless takeaway is a vital link to creating a wide power arc. Here's how to groove this action:

Set up with the butt end of the clubshaft in the center of your chest. Now rotate your shoulders in a clockwise position. Notice right away how your wrists remain tame. Visualize this move and watch how Tiger Woods does it in his swing. Now simply incorporate this takeaway action into your swing.

This drill will help you groove a wristless takeaway.

TIP #76:
ATTENTION: OVERWEIGHT GOLFERS

Overweight golfers tend to swing the club back too far outside the target line, then cut across the ball going through. The result: a weak slice.

To remedy this problem, exaggerate the clockwise turning actions of your shoulders. This will help you swing the club back on the inside, straight down the target line through impact, and back to the inside after impact.

TIP #77:
ATTENTION: TALL THIN
GOLFERS

Tall, thin golfers tend to pick the club up on a steep plane, then hit down sharply on the ball. You'll never hit powerful drives employing such actions.

To hit powerful drives, the club must stay low to the ground through impact. To promote a level flat spot in the impact zone, start off by keeping the club low to the ground in the takeaway.

TIP #78:
ROTATE YOUR
RIGHT SHOULDER

To hit more powerfully through the ball, rotate your right shoulder fully under your left shoulder in the impact zone, as the great Byron Nelson did during his heyday, and British Open champion Tom Lehman does today.

To encourage a powerful hit through impact, concentrate on rotating your right shoulder under your chin.

TIP #79:
LET THE KNEES
LEAD THE DOWNSWING

If videotape shows you overturning your hips on the downswing, spinning out, and hitting a short hook shot off the tee, stop thinking of unwinding your hips. Instead, concentrate on rotating your knees toward the target as you swing down. This knee action will put a governor on your hip turn, and help you hit the ball much more powerfully.

*On the downswing, it's vital to
rotate your knees toward the target.*

TIP #80:
THE PLANE TRUTH

In order to hit drives powerfully, you must swing the club down on a shallow plane. To establish this shallower angle of attack, keep your right elbow close to your side as you start down.

Coming into impact, keep your right elbow close to your side.

TIP #81:
ONE SINGLE SWING KEY

The typical high handicapper freezes over the ball because numerous swing thoughts swim around in his head. This obsession with mechanics causes tension in the hands and arms, and leads to a rigid swinging action.

Think only of driving the club low to the ground in the hitting area. This will take your mind off the start of the swing, plus ensure relaxation and powerful contact.

A good mental key is to think of the club coming into impact, in a streamlined fashion.

TIP #82:
SHOULDER–TURN TIP

To promote a powerful turning action of the upper body, rotate your left shoulder fully under your chin as you swing the club back.

*As you swing back, concentrate on turning
your left shoulder under your chin.*

TIP #83:
SPLIT–GRIP TRAINING DRILL

To learn the correct feeling of your hands and arms on the downswing, practice hitting shots with a split-handed grip (i.e., hands a few inches apart).

Grip normally. Incorporate this free-release feeling into your "real" swing and you'll hit powerfully accurate drives.

*This split-grip drill will help you groove
an uninhibited releasing action.*

TIP #84:
HIT THROUGH THE HOOP

Narrow holes, featuring hazards bordering the fairway, conjure up fright in the average golfer's mind. Consequently, he or she tenses up and mishits the shot.

To help take your mind off the hazards, think only of hitting the ball through an imaginary hoop a couple of feet in front of the ball. This will raise your confidence level, and allow you to employ a tension-free power swing.

TIP #85:
ASSUME A SQUARE SET-UP

If a hook or slice is costing you distance, set up "square": feet, knees, hips, and shoulders parallel to the target line.

A square set-up will help prevent mishits.

TIP #86:
WARM–UP DRILL

Oily muscles are essential to swinging powerfully. So warm them up by holding a club in the crooks of your arms, then turning back and through, in the manner shown here.

Use this drill to warm up your muscles,
so that they are readied for action.

TIP #87:
LET YOUR SHOULDERS
SWING THE CLUB INSIDE

Many amateurs make the mistake of swinging the club too far inside the target line on the backswing. This fault usually causes you to leave the clubface open at impact and hit the shot well right of target. If this is your problem, stop taking the club back with your hands and let the clockwise turning of your shoulders swing it inside.

Let your turning shoulders control the path of the club.

TIP #88:
PUT A STOP TO YOUR SWAY

If you sway your body to the right on the backswing, you'll find it difficult to time the downswing and hit with any real power. If a sway is costing you distance, set your right foot down with its toe end perpendicular to the target line. This set-up allows you to keep your weight on the inside of your right foot during the backswing, and turn around on the axis of your right leg.

*Set your right foot perpendicular
to the target line to prevent a body sway.*

TIP #89:
KEYS FOR PROMOTING A
POWERFUL UPSWING HIT

To encourage a powerful uppercut type action—club moving powerfully upward through impact—try to drive your left shoulder upward and hit against a firm left side.

As you come into impact, think of driving the left shoulder upward.

TIP #90:
EXTEND YOURSELF

To achieve good extension through impact and keep the club-face on the ball a split-second longer, try to straighten your right arm on the downswing.

Try to straighten your right arm on the downswing.

TIP #91:
UNIFYING THE HANDS

Many players with small hands lose the club at the top because they overlap their right forefinger over their left index finger. Take a lesson from Jack Nicklaus, a player with small hands who interlocks these two fingers. This change will allow for a good marriage of the hands, plus permit you to swing the club at maximum speed, while maintaining maximum control.

Players with small hands should try an interlocking grip.

TIP #92:
IF IT'S GOOD ENOUGH
FOR FRED COUPLES,
WHY NOT TRY IT?

If your left wrist is flat at the top of the swing, yet your drives aren't flying as far and as straight as you would like, allow your left wrist to be "cupped" in the manner shown in the accompanying photograph. The cupped position at the top (used by power hitter Fred Couples) opens the clubface, thereby allowing you to whip your wrists into the shot with no fear of hitting a wild hook.

If this "cupped" left wrist position is good enough for Fred Couples, it's good enough for you.

TIP #93:
HOW TO DROP THE CLUB INTO THE SLOT

To allow the club to drop down automatically into the perfect hitting position or "slot," push your right hip downward so that you feel pressure on the inside of your right foot. This will allow your right elbow to tuck into your side and the club to drop into the desired shallow downswing plane.

TIP #94:
ROOM TO MOVE

In order to generate power in the swing, your arms and hands must be given ample room to swing the club back freely. Coiling your right hip clockwise will help you accomplish this goal.

Turn your right hip clockwise for a freer arm-swing.

TIP #95:
UPRIGHT IS BETTER

An upright arms swing helps you create more power in the swing. Therefore, make the club travel in a longer arc by reaching for the sky, instead of swinging the club around you and keeping your hands low.

TIP #96:

REVERSE YOUR REVERSE

If you reverse pivot—shift weight to your left side on the backswing, to the right on the downswing—and lose distance, here's how to plug up this power leak:

Push the clubhead away straight back from the ball, with its sole practically brushing the ground. This move will trigger a wide swing arc, while at the same time forcing your weight to move correctly over to your right foot on the backswing. Just make a lateral shift with your hips at the start of the downswing, and your weight will shift nicely onto your left foot. The end result: more powerful drives.

A low takeaway will prevent a reverse-pivot action.

TIP #97:
PUT YOUR FOOT DOWN

If your backswing is so steep that you tend to hit down behind the ball and pop it up weakly into the air, keep your left foot down on the ground. This will promote a flatter swing plane and a powerful sweeping hit through impact.

*Some players swing better if they keep
their left heel planted or raise it slightly.*

TIP #98:
PLUG UP YOUR
POWER LEAK

If an early wristcock is causing power to leak out of your swing, swing the club back slightly outside the target line. This takeaway action encourages you to control the swinging action with the bigger muscles of your arms and shoulders (rather than your hands and wrists) and generates power more easily.

*Wristy players should try swinging the club
back outside the target line.*

TIP #99:
THE RIGHT STUFF

Unless you're very strong, avoid using a stiff shafted driver. Many amateurs choose a stiff shaft just to be "macho." That's foolish, because the stiffer the shaft, the harder it is to obtain height and carry on your drives. See your local pro and experiment with a medium flex shaft. You may find it easier to hit the ball farther more consistently.

A more flexible shaft may help improve your driving.

TIP #100:
BELLY–BUTTON TO TARGET

To encourage a powerful body turn through impact and hard hit shots, try and finish with your belly button facing the target.

To promote powerfully accurate shots,
try to finish with your belly-button facing the target.

POWER GAME NOTES

POWER GAME NOTES

POWER GAME NOTES

_____

_____

_____

_____

_____

_____

_____

_____

_____

_____

_____

_____

_____

_____

_____

_____

_____

_____

POWER GAME NOTES

POWER GAME NOTES

ABOUT THE AUTHORS

JIM MCLEAN is the Director of Instruction for KSL Properties' Doral Golf Resort and Spa in Miami, Florida, and PGA West/La Quinta in Palm Springs, California. Chosen 1994 PGA Teacher of the Year, Jim has instructed many of the top PGA Tour pros, including 1992 U.S. Open winner Tom Kite, Brad Faxon, and Peter Jacobsen. He is a Master Teaching Professional at *GOLF Magazine* and golf instructor for the Academy of Golf on The Golf Channel. He is also the Director of Instruction for the Chelsea Piers Golf Facility in Manhattan, New York.

McLean has written numerous best-selling instructional books, including *The Eight-Step Swing* and *The Putter's Pocket Companion*, and produced the highly successful videos *The X Factor* and *20 Problems/20 Solutions*. He has also lectured for the U.S. military and conducts numerous instructional seminars for the PGA. He resides with his family in Miami, and owns and operates the Jim McLean Golf Schools, headquartered at the Doral Golf Resort and Spa.

JOHN ANDRISANI is the senior editor of instruction at *GOLF Magazine*. He is also the co-author of several books, including *Natural Golf*, with Seve Ballesteros, *101 Supershots*, with Chi Chi Rodriguez, *Grip It and Rip It!* with John Daly, and *The Golf Doctor*, with Robin McMillan.

A fine player in his own right, Andrisani is a former course record holder and a former winner of the American Golf Writers' Championship.

JEFF BLANTON is a Florida-based photographer whose work has appeared in *GOLF Magazine*.